Marketing Your Book
Using the Internet

Marketing Your Book

Using the Internet

By

Cheri Powell

R. C. Linnell Publishing

Marketing Your Book Using the Internet

ISBN-10: 0984002596

ISBN-13: 978-0-9840025-9-7

Cover design by Dave Davis.

Published by:
R. C. Linnell Publishing
Louisville, KY 40205
www.LinnellPublishing.com

Other Books by Cheri Powell:
Seven Tips to Make the Most of the Camino de Santiago
(ISBN: 978-0-9840025-5-9)
Camino de Santiago Book of Days Flowers of the Camino
(ISBN: 978-0-9840025-0-4)
Camino de Santiago Book of Days Pathways of the Camino
(ISBN: 978-0-9840025-1-1)

Author contact information:
www.CheriPowell.com
email: info@LinnellPublishing.com

Acknowledgments

There are many people who contributed to the energy to get this book written and in print in a short period of time.

Cathy Fyock provided the original impetus when she asked me to create a webinar on marketing. I had given a class based on these strategies many times but never in webinar format. I decided to turn my notes into something more tangible to reach a wider audience. Thank you, Cathy, for suggesting it.

Eve Forbes, Leslie Moise, Mary Popham, Mary Ann Fitzharris and Selene Phillips gave their time and expertise reading the original drafts and giving me feedback on content, clarity, and grammar issues. Thank you Eve, Leslie, Mary, Mary Ann , and Selene for all your valuable input.

Dave Davis found inspiration in the topic and designed the cover art. Thank you, Dave, for your unbounded creativity.

My husband, Rick, supported me emotionally throughout the process. Special thanks and love to you.

Table of Contents

Introduction

When I first started writing this book, I considered calling it *A Marketing Guide for Introverts* because you will do most of the techniques without leaving your home. I quickly dismissed that title because anyone, not just introverts, can use these techniques and be successful in marketing books. And that's ultimately what all writers want: to get their words in front of readers.

The first step toward marketing a book is to make sure the book is ready to be marketed. The book should be free of grammar errors. Has it been edited by a professional? If it is fiction, are there plot, character, or scene issues? Has it been vetted by, not only family and friends, but by professionals and strangers who have no interest in flattering you? The book should be interesting and easy to read. If there are problems with the book, no amount of marketing is going to overcome them.

When you've written a really good book then you are ready to proceed.

Marketing is the art of persuasion. It is putting a product, your book, in the best possible light in front of people who have a high probability of buying it. Marketing is a variety of activities that indirectly contribute to a sale.

I'm going to teach you a little bit about marketing and a lot about how to think like a marketing expert. As you go through this book, think about how the individual strategies could be applied in slightly different ways. Your book is unique. Modify what is given here to apply to your situation.

There is a harsh reality in today's publishing industry: authors must do their own marketing. This is true whether you are traditionally published or self-published. Unless you have already sold a couple of million books for a traditional publisher, they will not spend money to promote your book.

A first time author, who has been picked up by a traditional publisher, must sell enough books immediately upon launch to pay back any up-front money, as well as all the expenses to bring the book to print. If not, the author may be dropped. Any royalty checks will be quite small.

Today's technology has made it possible to circumvent the old publishing rules. Your book does not have to immediately become a best seller. There are many books that continue to generate interest even though they have been on the market for several years. There are readers out there who don't care if a book has just come on the market. If it's a good book, they want to read it. Remember the tortoise and the hare? Who won in the long run?

These strategies can be used over and over again throughout the life of your book. Use them during your book launch. Use them when sales start to lag. A good book deserves to be read by many readers. Keep working at finding them.

The skills required to complete the strategies in this book are minimal. If you can use a search engine, follow instructions on web sites and write about yourself and your book, you will be able to execute the strategies. The necessary links and the logic behind each strategy is given. The application and use of each site is explained.

It is not necessary to become an expert on the functioning of every site. You will probably be familiar with many of the sites given. This book will teach you how to use a site to your advantage. If a particular strategy is working well for you, delve into it further to enhance that strategy for your purposes.

The techniques in this book will help you market effectively. I have developed them over several years to market my own book, originally published in 2006 as an eBook on a web site. I probably would have left it there forever, except the people running the web site decided to stop paying me royalties. They still sold my book, but I never saw another penny from those sales.

In 2010, I discovered Createspace and self-published an expanded version on Amazon. I now had complete control over royalties. I started learning ways to market the book. I received glowing reviews on Amazon and the book sold well. In 2012 I published a second edition, reflecting pertinent changes in the information. It continues to sell well.

The Internet is in constant flux. That's what makes it great. New sites pop up every day. Some are successful. Some are not. No one person can cover it all. What you can do is to become familiar with helpful sites and know how to use them well. This book will help you do that. Not everything in this book will work for everyone. I've tried to give a broad spectrum of ideas so you can select and act on the ones that make sense for you.

The first section in this book is "Information to Gather." You must have a solid grasp of who your readers are and what your book offers them or you will not be able to find them and persuade them to buy. Ideally, you are reading this before your book has been published. It will make many things easier. If you have already published, some things cannot be changed, but it is still possible to apply most of the techniques.

The "Internet Resources" section tells you how to use the information you've gathered. Most of it will be applied several times in different places. You can vary the format of some of the information depending on the site, but you need to have a rock solid understanding of the pieces of information and what they mean to your marketing effort.

As you read through the book, notice that I've given you an "Action Items" list for each section. This will force you to check off each completed step. No cheating. If you don't do something, don't check it as complete. Just reading this book won't get you where you want to be. Take action.

You don't have to do the techniques in the order they are presented. The one exception is your web site. If you don't yet have a web site, some of the other techniques will not work without a place to drive traffic to. Your web site also holds important information about you and your book.

Most of the strategies use free sites and materials. Those that do cost are shown with a dollar sign ($) after the site link. Some sites have both a fee structure and a free section. Those are indicated with $/F. As your sales grow, invest some of the profits to reach more people. If a particular strategy is not working, turn it off. There are no long-term contracts associated with any site.

I've also created a wider margin for notes, so that you can jot down ideas of your own as you are reading. Use this book as a workbook for your project. Highlight, underline, write in the margins. Make it work for you.

4

The average first time author, whether self-published or traditionally published, sells less than 200 books. If you use these techniques, you will multiply that number by many times. The more strategies you try, the more returns you will enjoy.

The sites mentioned will change over time. What works today may not work tomorrow. What I hope you will garner from this book is a way of thinking that will allow you to look at a new site and realize the potential. You will have new eyes and a new perspective.

Points to Remember

- ➢ The first step in marketing is to write a really good book.

- ➢ You will have to do your own marketing whether you are traditionally published or self-published.

- ➢ The audience for your book is out there. You can find them.

- ➢ No exceptional skills are required to execute the strategies.

- ➢ You do not need to be an expert on each site.

- ➢ The Internet will change. You will learn how to evaluate new sites for marketing potential.

- ➢ Strategies can be executed in any order after your web site is built.

- ➢ Most strategies are free.

- ➢ Use this book as a workbook.

Information to Gather

Before you can effectively market your book, there are pieces of information you need to gather to take the best advantage of the strategies. It's not a lot of information, but it does require some thought.

Sometimes the author of a book is too close to it to objectively come up with solid insight. So, this is an opportune time to gather friends and colleagues who have read the book and are willing to give you some honest feedback. Do you belong to a writer's group? Do you have friends who have read the book? Invite them over for a brainstorming session to talk about the items in this section. Buy some wine and snacks and make an occasion of it.

Listen with an open mind. Listen quietly and resist the urge to defend your book. The people you have included in your brainstorming session are representative of your potential readers. Their information is invaluable.

These tidbits of information are your building blocks for marketing successfully. Take your time until your gut tells you they are correct. You can do this. Take a deep breath. Here we go.

Title of Your Book

What is your book's title, or if you haven't decided yet, your working title?

_____

Is there a subtitle or tag line?

_____

The title of your book does not have to be unique. Your ISBN will differentiate your book from all others. Even though it does not have to be unique, you want the title to be associated with you and your book. You want to make it easy for a prospective reader to find. You must research what is out there now.

Enter your title in your favorite search engine. What comes up? Is it what you expected? Are the sites related to the topic of your book? This can be for fiction or non-fiction. If you are writing a children's book titled *Gregory's New Kitten*, what sorts of sites come up in a general search?

Now do the same search on Amazon. Is there already a book by that name? If so, you might want to consider changing yours so there is no confusion.

Search on the subtitle and tag line in the same way. What comes up? Other books? This could be your competition.

Work with the title and subtitle until you are happy with the types of sites and other books that come up with these same words. Remember, a potential reader will be entering these words in a search engine or in Amazon. You want to be associated with similar items or themes. It will make finding your book easier for readers.

Author Name

What author name will be listed on the book?

_____

This may seem like a silly question, but it is not. You want your fans to find your book. If you have a common author name, it may it more difficult. Say your name is Stephany King. Guess whose books are going to come up in a search with yours. You want your name to be unique.

You may be considering publishing under your initials. It worked for J. K. Rowling and P. D. James, but I'm not sure it would work for a new, untried author. Initials were used when it was thought the reading public would not read a book written by a woman. We know that is incorrect.

However, there is the dilemma of how your initials would be entered in a search field: JK Rowling, J K Rowling, or J. K. Rowling. James and Rowling are famous enough that search engines will not be confused. But for a first time author, each of these variations may produce different results. Most readers and potential buyers are not savvy enough to try all variations until they get it right.

If you have a common name or were planning to use your initials, I urge you to consider using a pen name or a variation of your name. Something still you but unique and easy for readers to find.

Your name as an author is the name you will use as you execute the strategies in this book. You will be this name on the Internet.

What is your book genre?

Fiction/Non-fiction

Category: _____

BISG code: _____

You need to know how your book fits into the publishing industry. Classifying your book will help put it in the correct places to get to your primary reader. There is a web site to help you figure this out. Go to https://www.BISG.org/bisac-subject-codes . This site is the Book Industry Study Group and they help classify books. Note that the site is an .ORG, not .COM. Scroll down the page to the BISAC Subject Heading List under "See below for more information" and click on it. You'll be taken to a list of classifications. Click on the one appropriate for your book. You'll go to an even more detailed page until you find the place where your book fits. There will be a number associated with the classification, such as FIC022070 for Mystery and Detective – Cozy.

Write this down, especially if you are self-publishing. You will need it when you submit information to your printer.

What is your book about?

_____

_____

In one or two sentences, explain what your book is about. This is your elevator pitch. For example, if you're in an elevator and someone discovers you're an author and asks, "What is your book about?" You have until the next floor to tell them. Practice this one. It is vitally important to answer quickly and make the book interesting. It's not as easy as it sounds. Work on it until it flows naturally.

When you have an elevator pitch you like, key the exact words into a search engine and see what pops up. This is what a reader might encounter if they did the same thing. Are you in good company? What sorts of sites or other books are on the search list? Is this what you want to be associated with? Do the same thing on Amazon. Ask the same questions. This will also tell you what your competition is.

Five Special Words

Five words for searching for your book:

_____ _____

_____ _____ _____

What would you enter to find new reading material? Think like a reader not a writer.

These are words or phrases a prospective reader might enter into the Amazon search or any search engine in an attempt to find a book to read. These will be associated with your book on Amazon and increase the chances your book will be high on the search list.

Technically these five items can be either a word or a phrase. However, if you use a phrase, it must match what someone types exactly to generate a hit. For example, if you choose "Kentucky folklore" for your book and someone enters "Kentucky," your book will not show on the list. If someone enters "folklore," your book will not show on the list. They would have to enter "Kentucky folklore" to generate your inclusion in the list. Be aware of how phrases work as you select the ones for you.

These Five Special Words are easier to find when you have a non-fiction book. A fiction book requires more thought. Some ideas might be a description of the topic of the book. You've written a story where the protagonist overcomes some emotional obstacle. Maybe one of your words is "emotional recovery." You've written a book about a pack of wolves whose behavior mirror the behavior of the human characters. Maybe one of your words is "nature."

Avoid words or phrases that are too generic. "Romance" is too common. "Forbidden romance" may be more appropriate. Try to look on the positive side of your topic. If your book is about a traumatic experience and how your protagonist overcomes the effects, go for "PTSD recovery" rather than just "PTSD."

To find out if you have chosen wisely, try them. Take each word or phrase and enter it in an Amazon search. What comes up? Books similar to yours? If so, then you probably want to use that word or phrase. Keep in mind that the first books to be shown are ones that have those words in the title.

Try the word or phrase in an internet search. You want to see the results that are associated with these words, because you are associating them with your book. That means that your book will be in the company of the sites that come up. Keep trying words or phrases until you find a fit.

Who will buy your book?

_____

_____

_____

_____

_____

Not everyone will read every book printed. To successfully market your book to readers who are interested and who will spread the word about your great book, you need to be realistic about its appeal.

Define up to five demographic groups of individuals who you think would be interested in buying your book. Be as specific as you can. Housewives. Hunters. Twenty-somethings. Think about age, income bracket, education, geographic region, job title or any other defining characteristic of your reader.

 If you're writing a cookbook, one group would be people who like to cook. The type of recipes you have – Italian, Greek, low-calorie, specialty – will further define the groups interested in your particular book.

If your book is a niche book, it may only have one major group of people who would be interested. That's fine. Just be aware of who it is.

If you are writing a fiction book, the task is a little more difficult but not impossible. If you write thrillers, go to your favorite search engine and enter something like "thriller novel readers demographics." If you write mysteries, you might try "who reads mysteries" as a search criteria. You'll get a list of sites with articles and information about the genre and who is reading it. With a little reading and deduction, you should be able to figure out the demographic being discussed. Write down the groups you discover.

What makes your book unique?

_____

_____

_____

_____

There are literally millions of books in print. What makes yours unique? Why would someone want to buy your book as opposed to all the others on the market? Your book could have a unique point of view. Are you telling a story to help others? Have you written a gothic fantasy spy novel that combines all the genres? Put some thought into this until you can articulate it without thinking. It will help you when you are filling out forms describing your book.

Action Items
Information to Gather

Remember: no cheating here. Don't just read this book. Put it into action. Do these things before you continue and everything will make more sense.

Date completed   **Item**

_____   Google the title and interpret the findings.

_____   Search for the title on Amazon to see if it is duplicated.

_____   Settle on a title and subtitle.

_____   Search for author name on Amazon and based on findings, settle on how name will be presented.

_____   Find a suitable BISG code.

_____   Be able to tell what your book is about in two to three sentences.

_____   Have five keywords for searching for your book.

_____   Have up to five demographic groups who would be interested in reading your book.

_____   Describe what makes your book unique.

Congratulations! You're on your way!

Internet Resources

Now that you have collected the necessary information, you have the building blocks to utilize the strategies given. The information will be used many times, in different ways. Sometimes modification may be necessary to make a particular piece of information work in a given site.

Not all of the strategies given will work for everyone. Part of your job is to evaluate the effectiveness of each one for your situation.

Amazon

Strategy: Establish a presence on Amazon with your information.

Amazon is your friend. The people running Amazon want you to sell books. When you sell books, you make money, and they make money. The site is for more than just showing your book. You can market from the site. The more information you make available, the more information a potential reader will see.

www.authorcentral.com

This is part of Amazon and is the place where you will enter all the information about you as an author. You will link your books to your author profile . You can create a blog, share events, and upload a video. Here's how to do it.

Log on to author central using your regular Amazon email log-in and password. If you want to create a special email for this purpose, then set up an Amazon account with that email. You want your name to be exactly as it is on your book. If you are using a pen name, a new Amazon account may be in order.

You will be taken to a "Welcome to Author Central" page, which will list several options. Click on the section that explains how to update your author page.

Your author page will appear. It has a place to add or edit your biography, to start a blog, to add events, to add an author URL, to upload your photo, to upload a promotional video, and to add your twitter account. Enter as much information as you can. It can be changed at any time you choose in the future. You want to keep this as current as possible.

When you have done this, click on the "Books" tab at the top of the page. This will take you to a page to allow you to associate books listed on Amazon with the information you have just entered. Click on the "Add more Books" button. It will take you to a search page. Enter the name or ISBN of your book. When it appears, click on the button to indicate this is indeed your book. Now when someone clicks on your book from a search list, your author information will be shown on the page.

Notice the "Sales Info" tab at the top of the page. Click on that, and you can review your sales over the past month. You can also view your book and author ranking on Amazon overall. These ranking levels change daily.

Now click on the "Customer Reviews" tab at the top of the page. You can see all the reviews written about your books. You can even give feedback to any review. If you get a low star review there is a temptation to comment and justify any negative feedback. Don't do it. Take the comment as a learning point, and keep it in mind for any subsequent books or any second editions you may write.

You have now updated your author page for Amazon in the United States. There is a separate Author Central page for Europe. It can be accessed at https://authorcentral.Amazon.co.uk. Use your same login and complete the pages in the same way so that sales in the European countries will see the same information about you. Currently, these are the only two author central pages available, although your book may be available on other Amazon sites.

As other Author Central pages are developed for other countries, Amazon will notify you. Log in and enter your information on each new page.

www.Amazon.com

There are some things that can be done on the regular Amazon page. If you haven't already done it, ask people who have read your book to review it online. A caution about this. Amazon scans for what it considers "fake" reviews and will remove them. The scanners look for uninspired reviews such as "A must-read book." Or reviews so general it is obvious that the person did not read it. So when you ask family and friends to review it, ask the ones who will give a truthful review. With work and a bit of luck, your book will take off and reviews will be coming in from everywhere.

While you're logged in, review some other books. This will give you a presence on Amazon. If you click on the "Your Account" tab at the top of the page, you will find a list of "Your" things. "Your Recommendations" will allow you to review books you have purchased. Go to any of the "Your" sites and review items purchased under music or video to add your reviews.

This will give you a presence on Amazon, and on the rest of the Internet as well, because the reviews are included in web searches. Make sure you use your author name when writing the reviews, so everyone knows you not only review books, you also write them.

When someone enters a search on Amazon, the computer executes a long, complex algorithm to decide the order to list the books. You want your book as high on the list as possible. But there are pages and pages of books listed. How can you get your book moved up on the list? There is a way.

Two of the factors in the algorithm are 1) activity on your book and 2) book sales. You can influence both.

Activity on your book simply means that searchers have clicked on you book title to bring up the specifics and have looked around the page, possibly bringing up the "look inside" feature. When this happens, the computer makes a note of what the search words were and the fact that your book was clicked on. The search engine is learning what words are associated with you book. You want to help the computer learn.

Your Five Special Words come into play here. Enter one of the words or phrases. Scan through the returned pages until you find your book. You may have to go twenty or thirty pages or more until you find it. Click on it. By clicking, you have just reinforced the association of one of your Five Special Words with your book. Bring up the "look inside" feature and click on a couple of areas featured. You've just told the computer that someone is interested in the contents of your book. Close the Amazon page. A few minutes later, go back on Amazon and do the same thing. Do not log in while you are doing this. The computer thinks another person is interested and moves your book up in the search results.

Do this as often as you can. When I take a break from other tasks, I'll casually bring up Amazon and search for my book using the words I want associated with it. I will look inside or go to the author page. All of these actions constitute activity and the search engine is taking note. You will notice movement of your book up the search return pages.

You may have the situation where you entered a word or phrase and your book did not appear even though you went to the end of the search results. Your task will be a little more difficult, but not impossible. Add your last name to the search words already in the field. Your book should pop up at the top of the list. Click on it. Click on "look inside" and read the first few pages. Close the Amazon page. Do the same thing again. And again. And again. You are associating one of your Five Special Words plus your name to your book. You are creating activity on your book page.

Do this for several days. Then enter the search words without your last name. The activity you've generated should be enough to have your book included without your last name. Continue the process you've been doing with now just the search words to move you up even closer to the top of the list. If you still can't find your book with the search words only, resume using your name until there is sufficient activity.

The other action that influences your place on the list is the sale of your book. Any time there is a sale, you move up in the ratings. I suggest you buy a couple copies of your own book retail in separate transactions. Use the search words, click on your book, and then buy it. You have doubly reinforced the association of your book to the search words.

When you buy your own book, use it for promotional purposes. You can write off the extra money you have paid as an advertising expense.

The combination of these two actions, searching and buying, will move you up on the search list no matter how long your book has been in print.

www.authormarketingideas.com

This web site was originally linked through author central, but it now seems to exist on its own. It is a compilation of articles and information about marketing your book. Check it regularly for new ideas.

Points to Remember

- ➤ Amazon wants you to sell books and will provide help.
- ➤ Your Author Central page allows you to manage information shown when someone clicks on your book.
- ➤ You can monitor sales through your Author Central account.
- ➤ Each of the different Amazon country sites has a separate Author Central page. Log in to each one to update your information.
- ➤ Reviewing other books on Amazon will help establish your name on the internet.
- ➤ You can influence where your book is listed on a search.
- ➤ The Author Marketing Ideas page is constantly displaying new articles with book marketing ideas.

Action Items
Amazon

Date Completed   **Item**

_____   Complete author bio on Author Central.

_____   Start a blog on Author Central.

_____   Upload a video, enter events and twitter account on Author Central.

_____   Claim books as yours on Author Central.

_____   Check out sales information on Author Central.

_____   Check out customer reviews on Author Central.

_____   Check out European Author Central for all features.

_____   Ask readers of your book for reviews.

_____   Review other books purchased on Amazon.

_____   Use your Five Special Words to help bring your book to the top of a return search list. Encourage friends to help.

_____   Consider buying your own book retail to raise your ranking on the search return list.

_____   Check out Author Marketing Ideas page.

Book Enthusiasts

Strategy: Get your book in front of avid readers.

www.goodreads.com
www.shelfari.com
www.librarything.com
www.bookbub.com

These sites are for readers who visit to find out what others are reading, to read reviews by others on the site, and to see what new books are being offered. Goodreads and Shelfari are now owned by Amazon, but they each serve a different function. There is still a close association with Amazon, the parent company. The other two are independent which makes navigating them different. Each site will allow you to establish yourself in the book reading world. Let's review them individually.

Goodreads

Goodreads started out as a site for avid readers. It still serves that purpose, but it is also a place for authors. Go to Goodreads.com and sign up for an account. You'll be asked a series of questions about your reading preferences. You'll also be asked to rate some books, and then other books will be recommended to you based on your preferences. When you get to the "Welcome to Goodreads" page, scroll down to the bottom and you will see a menu item titled "Author program." Click on it, and a page will appear that explains the program. You want to establish yourself as an author. There will be a "Join the author program" button. Click on that, and you will be directed to a page that explains the information needed to enroll in the program. Fill it out, and submit your application. You'll hear back in a couple of days.

While you are waiting to hear from them, fill out all the profile information and start joining groups. Join groups with an interest in the type of books you write. These are readers who may be interested in reading your book. Look at the demographic lists you made in the information gathering section of this book. Search to see if there are similar groups here and join them.

Rate some books you have read, and establish yourself on the site.

When you get your author approval notification, you'll now have an "Author Dashboard" added to your account page. Go through the author tutorial, and fill in any information not automatically entered for you. Link all your books to your dashboard. The tutorial will tell you how.

Scroll down the page. You can add a blog here. You can advertise your book. You can upload an excerpt from your book. And you can give it away. You want to give it away.

This may seem counter-intuitive. What you are doing is promoting your book. What better way than to let a few people read it and talk it up. You will ask for a review from them. If they like it, they will tell others. Word of mouth is the best advertising you can have.

To get listed in a giveaway, scroll to "My Books" and click on the book you want to give away. You'll see a box to the right listing "Author tools" and in that box is "List a Giveway." Click there, and you'll be asked for information about how many copies you want to give away, what dates you want for listing your giveaway, and what geographic areas are eligible. You can limit it to the United States, or Great Britain, or any particular country, or you can have it open to all. When you submit the information it may take a day or so before your book is listed as a giveaway.

People will read what you have said about your book and decide if they want to put their name in the drawing for the specified number of books you're giving away.

You can monitor the giveaway, and see how many people have signed up. At the end of the time frame you have given, Goodreads will draw the winners and send you the names and addresses of the people to whom you are to send a book. There are two different strategies you can use to fulfill the orders.

The first way to do it is to send a copy of the book from the supply you've received from your publisher. You can autograph the book. You can include a letter or note and ask the recipient to give a review on Amazon and Goodreads. I usually include a little caveat saying if you don't like the book, contact me at my email, and tell me why so I can improve it.

To send a book from your home, using your supply of books, you will have to pay for the physical book and postage. Keep track of this information, as it is deductable as an expense. I keep a tray in my office for Writing Expenses. When I send out a book, I print out the mailing address, and attach the postage receipt, add the price of the book, total it, and put it in the tray. It makes it easier to add up expenses at the end of the year.

The second way to fulfill this order is to go on Amazon and order the book retail. Mark it as a gift, and you can include a note asking for a review, and tell them you hope they enjoy the book. This will cost you more out of pocket, and it does something else for you. It counts as a sale on Amazon and will raise your standing in the search ranking. You will receive your normal royalty. The amount you spend for the book itself and shipping fees, minus your royalty, can be written off as an expense. Print out the sales information and put it in your expense tray. You don't have to go to the post office, and Amazon handles everything for you. I always use this method when sending books to another country. Go on the Amazon site for the country where the giveaway winner resides, order the book, have it sent as a gift and it will be cheaper than sending from your home country.

Shelfari

Shelfari started out with a mission similar to Goodreads; however, it has evolved to take over the "Lists" function that used to be on Amazon. This is where you can go and make lists of books to recommend to others.

Sign in using your Amazon account information and password. Review the information Amazon has supplied about you and fill in anything missing. Look under the "Profile" tab, and you'll see a section for "Groups." Once again, you can join interest groups. Do the same things you did for the Goodreads groups. You can now talk to readers interested in your type of books.

You can also create lists of books. Of course, you'll want to include your book in the lists you create so others can see where your book fits in.

LibraryThing

When you create an account at LibraryThing, you'll be asked many of the same questions for your profile.

To avoid wasting time, I keep a document of the most requested information, so I can cut and paste much of it. Once again, you can join groups, review books, and talk with other members via blogs. Use the same strategies you used on Goodreads.

BookBub

Bookbub is a place to cheaply buy books or receive them free. Once you sign up, you'll start receiving daily or weekly emails with lists of books you may be interested in based upon the preferences you entered in your profile. All the offerings are electronic and are downloaded into your Kindle or other electronic reader. But that's not your real interest at this site. You want to be an author giving away your book.

Scroll down to the bottom of the page, and you'll see a Publishers and Authors section. Take a look at the overview and the FAQ. This site is for promoting your book by giving away an electronic copy in a limited time frame. The people at BookBub will review your book, and if they find it acceptable, will list it in the emails delivered to thousands of people every day. Sounds great. But I know you don't want to give your book away to thousands of people. You want them to buy it so you will have some royalties. I agree.

The strategy for this site works best if you have more than one book for sale. You offer one of your books for free, and when readers click on the button to download it, they are taken to the Amazon, Barnes & Noble, Google, or wherever your book is listed. Your other books for sale will also be listed on the download page. The idea is that a reader will notice, and if they like your free book, will come back and pay money for your other books. Many authors are successfully employing this strategy.

If you don't have multiple books to sell, consider lowering the price and sell it for a very limited time. Any sale puts your book in a reader's hands.

Points to Remember

➢ Giving books away to interested readers may generate good reviews.

➢ Pay retail for any books you give away and increase your sales standing on Amazon. Write off this amount as an expense.

➢ Any lists you create on Shelfari will place your book in a similar group and thus increase your book's exposure.

➢ Joining groups in a similar genre will put you in the company of readers who like your genre.

➢ BookBub is most effective when you have more than one book for sale.

➢ BookBub can be effective for a single book by reducing the price for a limited time.

Action Items
Book Enthusiasts

Date Completed   **Item**

_____   Sign up for a Goodreads account. Complete your profile.

_____   Join the Author Program of Goodreads.

_____   Join appropriate groups on Goodreads.

_____   Rate books you have read on Goodreads.

_____   Create a giveaway on Goodreads.

_____   Sign in to Shelfari and join appropriate groups.

_____   Create lists in Shelfari.

_____   Create a LibraryThing account.

_____   Join appropriate groups in LibraryThing.

_____   Review books in LibraryThing.

_____   Sign up for a BookBub account. Enter your appropriate preferences.

_____   Submit your book for a giveaway on BookBub.

Your Internet Presence

Strategy: Establish your own place on the Internet. Use it to reach prospective readers, and send them to your Amazon listing to buy.

www.godaddy.com $
www.wordpress.com
www.bluehost.com $
topsitesblog.com/blog-websites/

A presence on the Internet is a necessity. A place where prospective readers can find out about you and your latest writing. The easiest way to do that is with a web page, a blog, or both. Your web site does not have to be elaborate, but it should be professional looking with persuasive information to encourage readers to buy your books.

You may hire someone to create your web page, or you can do it yourself. It will cost more to hire someone, but the professional appearance might be worth it. If you decide to do it yourself, there is still a cost involved, but it is minimal. Whether you hire someone or do it yourself, you will still have to pay for a domain name and a hosting service.

You do not need to have code writing skills to build a web page. The web builder software allows you do drop in text and pictures and position them on a page. If you can use a word processor, you can build a web page.

I'm not going into how to build your own web page. There are other comprehensive books available with a step-by-step process for getting it done. The web sites shown above will get you started.

Godaddy is probably the most well known place to buy your domain name. You can enter the words you want for your domain, and they will tell you if it is available. If it is not, try something else. You can also host your web site here. That means all the content for your site will be on their servers. They also have web page builders available. They are a little cryptic at first, but once you get the hang of how they function, you can manage your web page quite easily.

Wordpress is a software application web builder. To use it, you must already have your domain name and a hosting site. **Bluehost** is a hosting site that is Wordpress friendly.

Many do-it-yourselfers use the following strategy: Go to Godaddy to find out if your desired domain name is available, but do not buy it there. Go to Bluehost and buy the name from them. Also use Bluehost to host the Web site. Install Wordpress at Bluehost and build your site from there.

Whatever strategy you decide to use, have an idea in mind about the appearance you want for your site. Do a search for other author pages and when you find some you like, try to emulate the style, look, and feel of them.

The purpose of having a web page is so readers can find you and can learn more about you. You can have a blog directly on your web site. You can post excerpts from your books and list any upcoming events readers might want to attend. You should have a direct link to Amazon for purchasing your book. Whatever web builder you use will allow you to put links behind images or text. You can also link to Goodreads, Shelfari, or any other reading sites of interest.

If you decide to build the site yourself, be sure you find some literature on Search Engine Optimization, SEO. This is the process that makes it easier for readers to find you using search engines. Remember the Five Special Words you came up with in the Information Gathering section? This is one place where they are used. As you are writing the content for your site, use these words and phrases as often as possible without sounding forced. You want to have the words associated with your site so the search engines will put you higher on the search list. But your text must still sound natural for the topic discussed. You will receive a lower ranking if your site sounds amateurish, or "plugged" with certain words.

Make sure these words are in the metadata section of each page description. The individual web site builder you are using will have a place to enter them.

Activate the email address associated with your domain name and use it for all correspondence and anytime you need an email for any of the strategies in this book. It is more professional and will be accepted anywhere. At times, a free, internet based email such as Yahoo or Gmail are not accepted on some sites. More about this later.

QR Barcode

Strategy: Have an image for print material to take potential readers to your web site or Amazon page.

www.qrstuff.com

The Quick Response, or QR barcode is the cryptic looking little square that smartphones can read and will immediately display your web site, or any site you desire. They are a coded URL electronic devices can read.

Creating one is simple. Once created they are images in a .jpg format for putting on your business card, on the back of your book, in any advertisements you create, or just about anywhere your creative powers want to put them. And they are free.

The QRStuff site will allow you to enter any URL, and it will instantly create the barcode for you to download. It's that simple.

URL Shrinker

Strategy: Make the link to your Amazon page managable.

www.tinyurl.com
https://goo.gl – google URL shortener
www.bitly.com
www.webopedia.com/quick_ref/20-ways-to-shorten-a-url.html

Let's say you want to give someone a link to your book so they can purchase it. You bring up your book on Amazon, highlight the URL and copy (ctrl-C) and paste (ctrl-V) the link into an email. You notice that it is exceptionally long and unwieldy. No one can remember a long URL that doesn't make any sense. Wouldn't it be easier if the link were only a few characters long? Then you could easily put it on your business card or advertising and not have to remember so many characters.

It is also useful if you want to drive traffic directly to your Amazon page. There is usually a limit on the length of a URL in an ad. See the next section for more on this.

There are many sites that will give you a shortened URL you can use in any manner. This service is usually free. The sites listed here are some of the more popular ones.

Points to Remember

➢ A web site is a necessity. There will be some costs involved.

➢ You can create a web site inexpensively if you do some of the work.

➢ Search for other author pages to find a look and style you like, and then emulate it.

➢ Use your Five Special Words liberally on your web site.

➢ A QR Barcode can be added to any printed materials to promote or advertise your book.

➢ A URL Shrinker will make the link to your Amazon page easier to convey to others.

Action Items
Your Internet Presence

Date Completed   Item

_____   Decide on a domain name.

_____   Decide on a strategy for creating your
             web page.

_____   Create your web page.

_____   Activate the email associated with your
             domain name. Use it for all the strategies
             in this book.

_____   Create a QR barcode.

_____   Create a URL with fewer characters.

Driving Traffic

Strategy: Drive potential readers from a search engine to your web site or your Amazon page.

www.google.com/adwords $
www.google.com/alerts
Other Web Sites with common interest

Your ultimate goal is to sell books. Once you have your web page set up, you have a place to send any Internet traffic that inquired about your topic by entering one or more of your Five Special Words. The idea is that people using a search engine will be offered a list of sites, and you want them to go to your site. You can drive the traffic to your web site, which will have information about your book or you can drive it directly to your Amazon page using the shortened URL you have created.

There are several ways you may do this. I'm using Google as an example, because it is the largest and most used search engine. However, all search engines have something similar. If these techniques are working for you on this search engine, you may want to research the same types of functions on other search engines as well. Let's look at a couple of techniques.

Google Adwords

This one will cost a little money. It is the system associated with Google search. When you do any kind of search, there are a few sites listed at the top of each page or to the right. These sites have paid to be on a page when certain keywords are entered. Not every ad will come up in the same order every time the same search words are entered. You can decide how often you want to be on the list. You spend as much or as little as you think will be effective or can afford.

You pay a fee each time someone clicks on your ad. This is known as pay-per-click pricing. If the ad is displayed, but not clicked on, there is no charge. You will receive a monthly report via email telling you how many times your ad was shown and how many times it was clicked on. Start out small, and if you see a rise in sales, you may want to increase the frequency. If not, you may want to cancel. Here's how to do this.

Go to the Google Adwords link listed above. Read through the explanation on the page. It gives a good overview of what Adwords can do for you. Click on the "Start now" button. You'll be asked a series of questions to set up your account.

Finally, you'll be taken to a site to set up your campaign. This is the word for getting an ad shown as a search result. The Starter Campaign is a good way to try it out and see if it works for you. There are several pages of information to fill in to have the ad started.

The first is the ad itself. You have three lines plus a line for your URL link. Think through what you want to say to attract potential readers to buy your book. Remember the question, "What makes your book unique?" This is where you use that information. Using as few words as possible, fashion an ad that includes at least some of the pertinent information. Follow the site guidelines. Do not use words in all capital letters and do not use vulgar words. You may edit the ad at any time, but the ad will have to be approved by Google folks before it can go live. You can have more than one ad running at the same time. You can create different filters which will allow you to target your ad to better reach your market. These are controlled by the "segment," "filter," and "columns" buttons on the page. Starting out, you may want to take the defaults and refine it as you watch the traffic and see what works.

The next tab is "Keywords." This is where you enter your Five Special Words again. And you may enter more words and phrases. There is no limit, so enter as many words and phrases you think might generate a click. Remember, these words and phrases are what potential readers are going to be entering when searching for a topic. They may not necessarily be searching for a book. It will be the task of your ad, combined with your web page, if they click on your ad, to convince them to click on the link to Amazon to buy your book.

After your ad starts running, come back to this page and see what words and phrases are clicked on most often. You may even think of some more effective ones. Since there is no limit, use this to experiment and see which items create sales. If words are not getting clicks, change them, here and anywhere else they are used.

You may have your ad up and running with only the information you have entered. There are more refinements under the "Audiences," "Ad extensions," and "Dimensions" tabs. Take a look at those after you see how this is working for you.

I have found the customer service to be excellent. Don't hesitate to call them if you have any questions. They will walk you through the process. Just remember, they are trying to sell their service, so don't spend more than you are comfortable spending.

Google Alerts

This is a different service offered by Google and other search engines. It is free. This service will send you an email any time a specified word or phrase is used in a news item on the internet. It will tell you the title of the article and where it was published.

If your Five Special Words are specific enough, you can use them, or a phrase you came up with for your Adwords account. You want something precise enough to generate some hits but not general enough to overwhelm you.

My book is about the Camino de Santiago and that is the phrase I asked to be notified about. My topic is rather specific, so I don't get a lot of hits, maybe one or two daily. I look at each email to see if there is something I can use. I also have my name and the name of my book as words to be checked. So any time I am mentioned on the web or someone mentions my book, I am notified about it.

I am looking for several possibilities: 1) Is the publication or magazine that printed this article one that might print an article about my book or the topic of my book? 2) Might I want to send a press release in the future? 3) Is the article on a Web site or blog that might be interested in an article or a guest blog? 4) Is the author of the article someone who might write about my book? To figure this out, I scan the article and go to the home page for the publication or blog.

If it is a publication and it looks like I might want to submit an article for possible publication, I scan the page to find out the writer's guidelines. I have a few stock articles I can modify to fit the occasion and I submit one. The article itself is simply a way to have my bio printed in their publication. Make sure your bio contains the name of the book you are promoting. It is one more entry on the Internet containing your name and the name of your book.

If a press release is a possibility, I copy the link and save it in a document for this purpose. The next time I send out a press release for any reason, I make sure this publication receives a copy.

If it is a Web site or blog, I will send an email introducing myself and pitch the idea of being a guest blogger or having a link to my Web site or book. This will have to be customized for the situation. The objective is to get your name and the name of your book on another site. Ideally, there could also be a link to Amazon to buy the book.

I search the web to see if the author of the article has written other articles on the topic that links to my book. I find out what his or her interest was in writing the article that triggered the Google Alert. If there seems to be a pattern, I will email the author, introduce myself, mention the topic, and present my book as a possible topic for another article.

This process can be time consuming, and I don't do it all the time. I go in spurts when I have some extra time. Most of the Google Alerts I receive don't fall into any of these categories, and I just ignore them. However, the one that does fit may be a gold mine.

To set up your alerts, go to the Google Alerts link listing above. If you have a Google account and are logged in, you can start entering the phrases you want to be notified about. If you don't have an account, then create one now.

You'll be taken to a page with a field that says "Create an alert about...." Fill in the phrase you want and hit enter. Don't forget to create one for your name and the name of your book. That's it. Check your email for hits.

Other Web Sites

This strategy is a process of linking up with other sites. What you want to do is find sites that have some common thread with your book or with a demographic group that might be interested in reading your book. You do this by playing around with a search engine. I use Google for the examples, but you should try different search engines, because they often give different results when the same search words are entered.

For example, a friend of mine has written a book titled *Judith* about the biblical Judith who saved her village from invaders by exhibiting courage, cunning, and strength.

Who, specifically, might be interested in reading it? A couple of searches might be "women reading group," "Jewish reading group," "Christian reading group," "historical reading group," "historical book lovers," or "historical novel reading group." You get the idea. I scan the sites for about five pages of listings before I try another search. Often, I will print out the Google pages and check them off as I peruse them. Then I have a hard copy record of the sites I have contacted. I don't want to contact the same site on a subsequent day.

I am looking for web sites representing groups of readers or sites that may represent my book topic. Most sites have a "contact" page for reaching them. If a site representing the topic looks promising, I will send an email, introduce myself, and ask to put a link to my web site on theirs. I explain that my book may be of interest to people who come to their site, and that I am not competing with anything currently on their site. If it is a reading group, I will send an email explaining my book, and that their group might enjoy reading and discussing it. You might even have some discussion points ready that you will be willing to provide. You can also offer to be part of any meetings via whatever technology available.

You may think this sort of thing is intrusive. It is not. Anyone with a Web site wants to be found. I have been pleasantly surprised at the number of sites associated with groups and individuals who have responded positively to my request.

I wrote a couple of sample emails that I keep in a document that I can modify to fit a particular situation. I don't want to have to re-write them every time.

Do it a little each day and this task won't seem so overwhelming. You will be spreading the word about you and your book.

Points to Remember

- ➢ You want to capture any traffic in search engines that use your Five Special Words, and redirect it to your web site.

- ➢ Google Adwords charges fees on a pay-per-click system.

- ➢ A beginning campaign is easy to set up on Google Adwords.

- ➢ You can turn off Google Adwords at any time if you are not seeing an increase in sales.

- Google Alerts will notify you when specified words or phrases have been used in a news article on the Internet.

- You can review the Google Alerts you receive to see if there is the potential to submit an article, send a future press release, ask to be a guest blogger, or query the author of the article about writing an article about you.

- Other web sites with a theme or topic found in your book may hold potential for contacting interested readers directly.

- You can write sample emails for introducing yourself and you will not have to write everything from scratch each time.

Action Items
Driving Traffic

Date Completed   **Item**

_____   Set up a Google Adwords campaign.

_____   Set up Adwords campaign in other search engines.

_____   Write sample emails introducing yourself to send to other sites for a possible link to your site or your Amazon page.

_____   Set up aGoogle Alert for specified phrases.

_____   Set up Alert type accounts in other search engines.

_____   Write a sample introductory email to send to other web sites.

_____   Spend fifteen minutes a day finding web sites to contact.

Social Media

Strategy: Reach potential readers without spamming them.

www.facebook.com/ads $/F
www.linkedin.com/ads $/F
www.Youtube.com
www.pinterest.com

Social media has become a way of modern life. People spend hours on these sites talking to other people, posting things about themselves, watching others, and copying pictures from one place to another. Use this interest to your advantage.

Facebook is the granddaddy of social media. It has grown from its humble educational beginnings to a network linking people around the globe.

Of course, you can announce your book on Facebook and your announcement will go to all your friends. With a little luck, your friends will copy the announcement and pass it on to their friends. The copying will start to slow down pretty quickly.

If you have joined pages of groups that meet the definition of the demographics of your book readers, you'll be reaching your readership. Use demographic phrases and keywords to find possible groups and join them. You can announce your book or activities surrounding it as they occur.

Set up a professional Facebook page. It's free. You can establish yourself as an author and have more credibility to anyone viewing your page.

One way to reach a wider range of people is to advertise. Go to the link listed above and you'll see a good explanation of what they offer. You pay for the ad either when it is shown or when it is clicked on. Another pay-per-click system is in use here. You set a daily budget that will dictate how often your ad appears. You set up your target audience and your ad will appear to that audience only based on preferences each person defined in his or her profile.

Facebook gives a detailed explanation of how to set up an ad. Follow the instructions and guidelines.

Linkedin is the Facebook for professionals. It caters to people in business who want to network with each other. It is not designed for chatting or watching cat videos. If your book is business oriented, this may be a good place to announce when it is published. People who are linked to you will receive the announcement. If you want to reach a larger audience, you may also advertise here.

Ads are charged for on a pay-per-click basis. And again, you set a daily budget for the amount of clicks you want. You can target the ads to appear only on certain members based on a variety of demographics in their profiles. Go to the link above and read the overview of the process. If it sounds like this would work for your book, follow the steps on the site to set up your ad.

There is another way to find individuals who may be interested in your book. As on other sites, you want to join groups that share a common thread of interest with something in your book. You don't want to spam members of the group. If you have an announcement, book launch, or an event, then reach out to the members of the group with your announcement once, and only once.

You can also find prospects individually. To do this you must have a premium account, and this will cost you a monthly fee. You may try it free for one month. I'd recommend trying the free month when you have time to devote to it to see if it is worthwhile before spending the monthly fee. You might be able to generate enough leads during your free month and you won't need to continue this process indefinitely.

At the top of the page, next to the search field, there is an "Advanced" button. Click on it, and a window will open up with some different search options. Use the Keywords field to enter your Five Simple Words, one at a time. You'll see a list of people each time. You can also enter any phrases that might find people who would have an interest in your book. Do the same thing in the "Interested In" field on the right of the screen.

You want to reach out to each person individually. Do not just hit the Connect button and send the generic message asking them to link with you. Click on the downward arrow and select the "InMail" function.

You will be allowed to enter a personalized message to this person. Compose a carefully worded message that mentions the thing you have in common (what you searched on) and the fact that you have something (your book) they might find of interest. Invite them to link to you and your page.

You must be sincere in your message. You don't want to spam members. LinkedIn will take action if someone complains about your actions.

By doing this you gain a following and you sell some books. Your following will be useful for any future announcements.

YouTube is useful if you like to make videos. You can hire someone to make a Book Trailer for you. These are similar to Movie Trailers, but they promote your book. If you make one, it can also be uploaded into your Author Central page and your web page. If this idea appeals to you, search for "make a book trailer" and you will be presented with many sites either offering to make one for you or giving you instructions to do it yourself.

Pinterest is a site where members share pictures. Surprisingly, I have found it to be the most useful social media for promoting a book. The site is used in conjunction with your web page to drive interested people to your book. Let me explain how this works.

You must have your web page in place with a link to your book on Amazon. Join Pinterest. The idea behind Pinterest is that you want to pin things to a board so you may look at them whenever you want. You create "boards" that have a theme of some sort, so all things pinned on a given board go together somehow. You can be quite creative doing this. The beauty of it is you may pin things on your boards from other people all over the world. If you find an image you like on someone else's board, you pin it to yours. By doing so, you've created a link between your board and the board where you originally found it.

You can also pin images to your board from any page on the internet. Download the "Pin it" icon to your web browser. When you sign in, the first display page will have a button to download the icon. When you go to a web page and see an image you like, click on the icon, and it will allow you to capture any image on the page.

Create images on your own web page to pin on your boards in Pinterest. That way, anyone who re-pins your images will create a direct link back to your web page.

The catch here is that you want to create inspiring images people will want to duplicate on their boards. Look around at some other boards, and you'll see many with inspiring writings on them. These are popular and are re-pinned many times. You want to do something similar.

Start a board with something from your book: the theme, the setting, the characters, the genre, or anything that might complement your book. Do a search on whatever you've titled your board, and see how many others have a similar one. Re-pin some images you like. You might even see some other books being promoted and be inspired by them.

Now create some images you can put on your web site, then pin to one of your boards. Be creative.

You can use MS Word to create these images. Open a document and set the paper size to the size you want your image to be. Insert any photos or artwork you like. You can also use the "background" function to give color to the image. Type in any text you want. Put an image of the cover of your book in one corner. Put your web site URL across the bottom. It won't be clickable, but it will be there. Save the document.

You've created a .doc or .docx formatted image. It should be in .jpg format. There are a couple of ways to change it. Open it and center it on your screen. Use the "prt scr" button on your keyboard and you will have the complete screen in .jpg format. You need to crop out everything but the image you want. Any photo editing software will do this. Many can be downloaded for free.

Another option is to download Picpick.exe. It's also free and will let you pick only the area on the screen you want to capture.

Now you've got a .jpg formatted image. Upload it to your web site in some sort of context. You might have a page of these images surrounding the cover of your book. Pin it to one of your boards on Pinterest. With a little time, your image will be copied many times by people who have an interest in the topic of your board, which translates into an interest in your book.

Points to Remember

➢ Joining groups with similar demographics to your readers on all social media will put you in touch with potential purchasers of your book.

➢ You can advertise on most social media sites.

➢ You can also approach individuals who fall into the demographic characteristics of your reader.

➢ Be careful how you approach individuals. Make sure there is a common interest and point it out in your message to them.

➢ Pin images on your web site to your boards on Pinterest.

➢ You can create attractive images using MS Word.

Action Items
Social Media

Date Completed   **Item**

_____   Open a Facebook account and accumulate friends.

_____   Announce your book or event on Facebook.

_____   Join groups on Facebook.

_____   Advertise on Facebook.

_____   Open LinkedIn account.

_____   Join groups on LinkedIn.

_____   Open a free premium account for one month.

_____   Use advanced search and Five Simple Words.

_____   Reach out to five people a day.

_____   Open a YouTube account.

_____   Create and upload book trailer.

_____   Open a Pinterest account.

_____   Create boards with some connection to your book.

_____   Create images connected to your book, and place them on your web site.

_____   Pin your web images to your Pinterest board.

Press Release

Strategy: Announce newsworthy events about you and your book.

Press Release Distribution services
www.freepressrelease.com/
www.prlog.org/
www.prweb.com
www.prfree.com
www.pr.com
www.prnewswire.com $
www.pitchengine.com $
www.send2press.com $
www.24-7pressrelease.com $/F
www.gebbieinc.com $
www.avangate.com/company/resources/articl
e/press-release-distribution.htm

Newspaper Lists
www.usnpl.com
www.onlinenewspapers.com
www.bookbloggerdirectory.wordpress.com

There are times when you want to announce something to the world: your book launch, a book signing or reading, or the fact that you'll be at a specific place selling your book. To get the word out, you can use a press release hoping a publication will pick it up, call you, write an article, and include it in the next issue.

So how do you get the word out? If your event or announcement is local, you can send the release directly to local newspapers, magazines, and other publications. You may either write the release yourself or pay someone to write it. Press releases have a strict format and one written by a novice will not garner the attention a professionally written one will receive.

To learn the required structure, search for "press release format" or "press release template" and many sites will pop up. Click on a few until you find one you like. Follow the formula and write up your announcement.

You want to send your press release to the appropriate journalist. To find the appropriate journalist, go on the web site for each local publication and look for a "Contact Us" link. It is usually at the bottom of the homepage. It will list the editors and journalists of the different information areas. If none fit your requirements, send the release to the general editor.

The press release should be cut and pasted into the body of the email. In the subject line, put the title of your press release. Do this for each publication. Send individually to each one, not a list of newspapers in your "To" field. Each editor, news director, or journalist likes to think they are receiving an original release.

If you are announcing an event and want to be listed on the public calendar of the publication, you can be more direct. Send an email to the person who manages the calendar, and ask directly to have your event included. This may meet with more success than a press release.

That's fine for a local event, but if you are announcing a book launch, you want to try to reach a wider audience. You need a press release distributor. There are many, and most are specific in distribution or theme.

The sites listed at the beginning of this section will distribute a press release you submit to their subscribers. Not all press release distributors go to every publication. There are too many publications with too many different reader demographics. When you go on the distribution site, look at what publications they distribute to. Are these the publications you want to reach?

Some of the distributors charge a fee. Take a look at where they distribute to evaluate if the fee is worthwhile. Many who charge a fee also have a free service that is not as expansive as the paid versions. Check it out. The free version may be sufficient.

Most of the distributors have a fill-in-the-blank page for receiving your press release. If you've written you press release according to the format guidelines, this will be a matter of cutting and pasting. It is not difficult to do. The editors will review it for compliance with their guidelines and notify you when it is sent out.

The list given here is not inclusive. Use any search engine to find distributors who may be more attuned to the theme of your book.

There is no guarantee your press release will be picked up. It may just be bypassed as not news worthy. Journalists are looking for something to pique the interest of readers. An angle. A hook. Something. Otherwise, it is not worth the journalist's time to contact you, solicit the information, and write an article. You've just published a book? Who cares? It's your job to link the launch or event to something newsworthy.

The best way to get a journalist's attention is to tie something in your press release with a recent trend, a recent news event or something seasonal, or around a holidays.

For example, you've written a novel about a vampire who discovers she's also a werewolf. Around Halloween, you might title a press release "Author combines vampires and werewolves in one unforgettable character."

Say you've written a garden book about the life cycle of wildflowers. In the spring you could send a press release titled, "New book details wildflower life cycles." It may not sound interesting to everyone, but sent to a garden journalist, it could inspire an article.

Maybe your book is set on Cape Cod. A press release might be titled, "Author inspired by tranquility of Cape Cod beaches."

You get the idea. There has to be something more than the launching of your book or a book signing event to create interest. If you're trying to revive sales of a book that has been on the market for a while, watch the news for any tie-in that you could relate to your book.

One caveat here: many distributor sites will not send out a press release if your email is from a free, online site like yahoo, gmail, hotmail, or any of the Internet providers. You should be using the email associated with your web site with your domain name as the server.

If you want to take a more direct approach but still want to reach an audience in another geographical location, you can search several sites of lists of newspapers. **USNPL** lists newspapers by state, then city. You can get the address, phone number and link to the newspaper web site.

Online Newspapers lists newspapers worldwide. If your book has an appeal in another country, check out this list. Many foreign newspapers have an English version. If not, there are translation services available to translate your press release. Search for "language translation services.

The Book Blogger Directory is a place to find a blog about books. If you have a blog, you may want to be listed here. If you want to be a guest blogger on someone else's blog, here is the place to find them.

There is one more thing you should have to make it as easy as possible to interview you: a press kit. A press kit consists of items a journalist needs to write an article about you and your book. If a journalist calls you because of a press release, you can send him or her your press kit. It will give the journalist the necessary background information to begin the article. He or she can call you for any other information.

A press kit consists of:

o   An author bio,

o   An author photo – color and B&W versions, high resolution and low resolution,

o   Front cover of your book for inclusion in an article,

o   Author interview questions – typical interview questions already answered,

o   One to two page synopsis of your book,

o   Any inspirational, unusual characters or settings that provide background about your book, o Copies of any book reviews,

o FAQs – if your book typically raises question, what are they and what are the answers,

o Fact Sheet – more for non-fiction – any interesting facts about your book topic, and

o Your contact information or business card.

All of this information can be put on your web site under a "Press Room" or "Media Room" tab. or it can be physically printed and sent to a journalist via snail mail. If you decide to print it on paper, make sure it is professionally done. Don't just type it up and print it out. Have headings, use different fonts for headings and text to make it readable, and print it on quality stationery.

Points to Remember

➢ A press release has a specific format. Learn it.

➢ Find the appropriate journalist at a publication by finding the "Contact Us" page.

➢ Send press releases about a local event directly to local publications.

➢ PR distributors will reach a wider range of publications.

➢ If a distributor sends to publications with the same readership as your book, it may be worthwhile to pay.

➢ To make your press release newsworthy, tie it to a recent trend, recent news, something seasonal or concerning a holiday.

➢ Use a contact email associated with your domain name, not an Internet freebie.

- ➢ Find newspapers in other areas by using one of the newspaper sites above.

- ➢ Find bloggers on the blog list site above.

- ➢ A press kit will make it easier for any journalist who wants to write an article about you.

Action Items
Press Release

Date Completed   **Item**

_____   Learn the required structure for a press release.

_____   Distribute your press release to local publications.

_____   Distribute your press release to free online distributors.

_____   Find blogs with a theme or interest compatible with your book.

_____   Have yourself photographed for a press kit.

_____   Write your author bio for a press kit.

_____   Write up and answer typical interview questions for a press kit.

_____   Write synopsis of your book for a press kit.

_____   Write background for your book.

_____   Format reviews, feedback, and comments on one document for a press kit.

_____   Create a FAQ sheet.

_____   Create a fact sheet about your book.

_____   Create a contact information sheet.

_____   Have business cards printed.

_____   Press kit is complete!

Miscellaneous

The following topics don't fall into any special grouping. They represent a few more strategies to add to your arsenal of techniques.

Web Sites for Writers

Strategy: Solicit feedback on your book and your writing.

www.thenextbigwriter.com $
www.writerscafe.org
www.critiquecircle.com $
www.autocrit.com $
www.writersdigest.com/101-best-websites-for-writers

There are a variety of writing web sites available. These sites are of interest to writers, not readers. Each one offers a list of services available. The biggest service they provide is feedback on your writing from a writer's standpoint. If you have not yet published, these sites are a wonderful resource to help polish your prose.

You are probably reading this book because you've already published yours. Keep these sites in mind for your next book.

Some have a fee to join. Some are free. The list above is only a starting point. Search for "writing websites" to find many more.

The Next Big Writer offers an annual contest for the best start of a novel. You submit the first three chapters of your book, and it is judged by experts at the site. You could win a publishing package. At the very least you'll receive some valuable feedback. You can also submit portions of your book for feedback from other members. To do this, you must also give feedback to others. They have a system whereby you earn and spend points, depending on how much feedback you give.

Writer's Café and **Critique Circle** are similar sites. You can submit work and receive feedback from other members. They offer contests and have information about publishing. Check them out.

AutoCrit is unique. It will give you automated feedback on your writing. I use this while I am in the process of writing. It catches grammar issues and writing pitfalls. It has helped me rid myself of some bad writing habits – repeated words, too many adverbs and overuse of the word "that." You'll have to pay to join, but it is well worth it.

Writer's Digest's 101 Best Websites for Writers is updated annually, and it is a good way to discover sites of interest. You can spend hours perusing the sites. Just don't get too involved and forget to do some actual writing.

Points to Remember

➢ Writing websites give valuable feedback on many levels.

➢ AutoCrit gives automated feedback on grammar and many writing problems.

> Writer's Digest has compiled and reviewed many interesting sites for writers.

Online and Hardcopy Publications

Strategy: Find publications with readers similar to your reader demographics. Submit articles. Revive lagging sales.

www.WritersMaket.com $/F

There are thousands of magazines in existence. Many are only electronic. Many are only hard copy print. Many are both. You want to find the ones with a readership similar to your reader demographics. Go through the Writer's Market database, online, or the print version. There is a fee to use the database online. Most libraries carry at least one copy of this valuable book. It's worth it to check it out or spend an afternoon looking through it in the library. I like my own copy so I can write in the margin and turn down corners. Used book stores sometimes have older editions at a reasonable price. They are is still current enough to be useful.

To use this strategy successfully, you have to shift your writing style a bit. You've written a book you want to promote. Now you're going to write articles about some aspect of your book and submit them to magazines, online and in print.

Scan the "Consumer Magazines" section for magazines with a similar readership to your book. You'll want to write an article of interest to the magazine readers. Check the "writer's guidelines" for each magazine. They will be different. Be sure to follow the guidelines to increase your chance of being published.

Write and submit your article according to the guidelines.

This is a tedious step. It is out of the comfort zone of most novel writers. However, it can be productive when trying to revive sales for a book that has been on the market for a while. Each time you publish an article, your bio will have the name of your book. If readers liked the article, they may buy your book. And it is another place where you have established yourself as a writer.

Points to Remember

➢ Submitting articles to magazines with similar readership is a good way to get your name and book in front of potential readers.

➢ There is probably at least one magazine with a readership similar to your reader demographics.

➢ Submitting articles is a good way to revive lagging book sales.

➢ Writing articles may be out of your comfort zone, but the effort can pay dividends.

Direct Online Sales

Strategy: Sell your book directly to individuals.

www.ETSY.com $
www.EBay.com $
www.PayPal.com $

ETSY has become one of the largest sites for hand-made items in the world. That can be a good thing, because your product has the possibility of being viewed and purchased by millions of people. It can be bad if you get lost in the clutter.

You may not think of this as a place to sell your book, but it is. There is a category for books, movies, and music. You will find many things listed. I keep a copy of my book for sale here. I don't get a lot of sales, but I do get some.

When you register with ETSY for the first time, you will fill out a profile and give your credit card information so you may buy items on the site. You must provide an email address to be used for your communication. They will send a confirming email to you. Open it, and click on the confirming link. You're in.

You'll be taken to the ETSY home page. Scroll down to the bottom menu and on the far left you'll see an "Open a Shop" button. Click it. You get an explanation of how they work. Click again on the "Open a Shop" button, and you'll be led through a series of questions about what you want to sell. They want a shop name, a description of goods, and a few other things. Once this is set up, you won't have to go through it again.

When your shop is set up, you can list items for sale, namely your book. It will cost about twenty cents to list a copy, and there is a small fee when it sells. You will receive an email for each sale telling you the name and address of the person who bought it. You are responsible for getting it to them. The money they paid is deposited in your PayPal account.

When you are filling out the description of your book, do not forget the Five Simple Words. Make sure you use them liberally in your shop and on the individual book description.

EBay is similar to ETSY in a lot of respects. The one big difference is eBay is an auction site and requires more attention to keep a book listed on it. Registration is easy. When you go to eBay.com you'll see a "Sign in or Register" button in the upper left. Click "Register." You'll be asked to give your name, an email address, and a password. You are immediately set up with an account. You can now buy items. But you want to sell.

Notice a menu directly below the URL field. There's a "Sell" item. Click it, and you will be asked more information to set you up as a seller. It's all pretty straightforward. You'll have to be approved to sell. You do not need to have a business account. Those accounts are for high-volume merchants that are truly stores that sell hundreds of items a day. You only want to sell your book here. After you see how easy it is, you may decide to clean out your attic.

If you decide to use ETSY or eBay, you will need a **PayPal** account to collect the money. The home page of the site gives an explanation of how it works. It's basically an online bank. To open an account, click the "Sign Up" button at the top of the page. You want a personal account not a business one. You give your email account and create a password. This should be the same email that you used to set up your ETSY and eBay accounts. They will deposit your money from sales directly into this account. You can leave it there and use it for purchasing items, or you can transfer the money to your bank. All is explained in a straightforward manner on the site.

I've spoken to some people who are leery about using an online site to hold money. I've used it practically since they opened their electronic doors and I have not had any problems. If it makes you nervous, simply spend the money or transfer it as soon as you earn it.

Points to Remember

➢ ETSY will get your book online worldwide.

➢ It costs nothing to open an ETSY shop and only twenty cents to list an item for sale. Another small fee is taken for each book sold.

➢ It is easy to open an eBay account and be approved to sell items. A limited number of items can be listed with no fee. A small fee is taken when the item is sold.

➢ You will need a PayPal account to sell on ETSY or eBay.

➢ PayPal is safe and easy to use.

Reviewers

Strategy: Get professional feedback to promote your book.

www.kirkusreviews.com $
www.AmericanBookReview.org
www.newpages.com/faq

Nothing warms a writer's heart more than a good review. Nothing can bring on symptoms of depression faster than a bad one. We all want to feel good about what we have created. A good review on Amazon can lead to more sales.

Reviewing books has become big business. A search of "book reviewer" will bring up several pages of reviewers who are more than willing to review your book for a price. Be wary before you spend money. Some of these reviewers are legitimate and know how to review a book. Others are only out to make a buck. Check out the credentials of anyone you are considering using. Ask to see some posted reviews and read them carefully. Make sure the reviewer is familiar with your genre. Find out every place the review will be published. Make sure it will reach the audience you want. Finally, ask to see the review before it is posted. If the review is less than favorable, you may not want it published.

One of the most famous reviewers is **Kirkus Reviews**. Kirkus employs professionals who have been doing reviews for years. If your review is three stars or less out of five, they will contact you about not publishing it. Kirkus reviews are usually done before publication. The review or quotes from it may be included on the book cover. Kirkus have their own publication where your review will also be printed.

Before you spend money on a review, think about who will read it and if a review by this person or organization will influence readers. Do your reader demographics indicate they will be influenced by the reviewer?

Other options are the **American Book Review** and **New Pages** publications. You can submit a copy of your book, either before or after publication and they may review it and put the review in their publication. You will be notified if your book is selected for review. It's worth a try.

Points to Remember

> A good comprehensive review may lead to more book sales.

> Check out thoroughly any reviewers you pay to review your book.

> A Kirkus review will be objective. It will also be expensive.

> American Book Review and New Pages allow you to submit your book. They may or may not review it.

> Any reviews can be used as marketing tools.

Celebrity Endorsement

Strategy: Get an endorsement or recommendation from an influential person.

The Celebrity Black Book
www.ContactAnyCelebrity.com $

Is there a celebrity or well-known influential person who has an interest in the theme, topic, genre, character, or any aspect of your book? If so, you may want to try to get an endorsement from this person. Any quotes he or she give you can be used on the back of the book or in promotional or advertising materials.

If you don't have a contact or relationship with someone who does, you can try contacting them directly. *The Celebrity Black Book* published by Mega Niche Media and their corresponding web site ContactAnyCelebrity contains the most comprehensive list of celebrity addresses. Sometimes the address listed is for the person's agent. Keep that in mind when writing the letter.

Choose your words carefully when writing to a celebrity. Introduce yourself, and explain why you are writing. Mention the common interest or topic you have with them. Be specific about what you want from them. Is it a comment to print on the back of the book? Would you like them to write a forward to the book? Do you want to mention them when advertising your book?

Be sure to point out what the celebrity would receive for doing this. For example, are you writing a novel about wolves and this celebrity is known for his or her work in conserving wolf habitats? Make sure there is some connection to urge the celebrity to consider your request.

Points to Remember

➢ An influential person who endorses your book can lead to higher book sales.

➢ Carefully craft your letter to a celebrity or influential person. Be specific about what you want.

➢ Give the celebrity or influential person a reason to endorse your book.

Contests

Strategy: Add any acclaim and publishing credibility to your book cover. Win money and/or prizes.

www.readersfavorite.com
www.writersdigest.com
www.independentpublisher.com
www.indieexcellence.com/
www.nautilusbookawards.com/

There are many contests available for published books. Search for "book contest" and you'll see pages and pages of sites. I am familiar with the ones I have listed, and know these are reputable. Many are not.

When deciding if a contest is for you, there are several factors to consider. The crucial one is: Would winning this contest impress potential readers and influence them to buy your book? To answer, you need to know your reader base. If you are a first-time author, winning a recognized contest will add credibility to your writing ability. It may also gain you many additional readers.

Before entering any contest, be sure to check out the credentials of the contest organizers. How long has the contest been in existence? Is your genre well represented? Are you familiar with the previous winners of the contest? What is the actual prize? Money? Publishing deal? Marketing? What are the odds of winning?

Find out if anyone has had a bad experience with this contest. Search for "'name-of-contest' feedback" and see what comes up. I've seen many angry posts by people who spent money to enter the contest and after winning, learned it was a sham and no real awards or prizes were given, or the prize was not what was stated on the entry form. Stick with reputable contests.

Most contests require an entry fee. This is usually at least $100, so entering multiple contests can become expensive rapidly. Choose carefully.

Points to Remember

➢ There are many contests for newly published books.

➢ Not all contests are reputable. Check all credentials before entering.

➢ Evaluate whether winning the contest you enter will increase book sales.

Publicity

Strategy: Get mentioned in the news.

www.helpareporter.com

Publicity is defined by Google as "the notice or attention given to someone or something by the media." This attention may be good or bad. You want to attract the good kind.

Many of the activities in this book may result in publicity as a byproduct. Winning a contest, getting your book reviewed, and having your press release picked up will all generate some form of news about you and your book.

There is another, more direct way to possibly be included in articles and news items. Did you ever wonder where writers of magazine articles find their examples? They may be assigned to write on a topic and will want real-life examples to illustrate their points. Many often turn to the Help a Reporter web site.

This site regularly has requests from reporters and other writers to find experts in a field or people in a certain situation who they can talk about in their article. You sign up to receive emails on requests reporters have made. If you fit a request, contact the reporter with your information. This may entail writing a paragraph or two about how you fit the request. If the reporter likes what you have written, he/she will contact you for more information and possibly use you in the article.

What your book is about and any expertise you have will determine if this is something you should pursue. It only takes a couple of minutes each day to review the email with the requests. You may discover you fit a request that has absolutely nothing to do with your book. That's okay, it's still publicity.

To sign up go to the **Help a Reporter** home page. Click on the "Sign Up Today" button and you're taken to a page which lists the fees for services. Scroll down, and you'll see a free service for the emails. Click on that and sign up for just the emails.

If you are expert on a subject, it may be worth paying for a more advanced account.

A link to your press kit will be useful to send with your response to anything in the emails.

Points to Remember

➢ Publicity is like free advertising.

➢ Help a Reporter is an easy way to see what reporters are requesting.

> ➢ Help a Reporter is easy to sign up for.

> ➢ Your press kit is useful here also.

Book Fairs / Events

Strategy: Sell your book directly to event participants. Hand out promotional items.

www.eventcrazy.com
www.festivalnews.info

Book fairs seem like the logical place to sell books. People who attend are looking for something to read, and you have books to sell. Every year, there are hundreds of book fairs across the country. And they are easy to find.

A simple search of "book fairs" will yield several pages of sites. Add the name of your city to the search criteria, and it becomes more specific to your location. It is your job to evaluate how useful a book fair will be to your overall sales.

Book fairs charge a fee for setting up at their event. Calculate how many books you will need to sell to cover the fee and any other expenses you may incur while participating in the fair. Will you make a profit? Do you need to supply your own tables or tents? This can be an added expense. Will you spend the night in a hotel? Another expense to subtract from possible sales.

It may still be worth it if you participate in the fair to publicize your name to the reading public. You can hand out bookmarks and business cards with information about your book. You can give away CDs with the first chapter of your book. You can hand out hard copy of the first few pages or even the first chapter. If your writing is compelling, they will want to read the rest of your book. You can auction off one or two copies of your book and thereby gain names and emails of prospective readers.

Large fairs in major cities will draw thousands of people, but the price of a booth will be several hundred or even several thousand dollars. Find out if your publisher is going to participate and if your book can be included in that booth.

Book fairs typically have criteria to be included in the fair. They want the most recently published books. They may have restrictions on themes or genres. Make sure the fair is a fit for you and your book.

Another possibility for selling books is to set up a table at other types of events not specifically associated with books. Local fairs and festivals may be good choices depending your reader's demographics. If you have a niche book, only appealing to a specific audience interest, this may not be the best way to reach your reader. However, if you have a general interest book, it may be worth a try.

The two sites listed above are good for finding events. You can go to the sites and look at upcoming calendars. To find more possibilities not listed at these sites, Search for "events in name-of-your-city" and see what pops up. Also try "festivals fairs in name-of-your-city." You get the idea. You should have many sites to evaluate.

Not all events will let booksellers participate, simply because of the nature of the event. Most events have a web site with information about the demographics and number of people who attend. Compare with your reader demographics.

These types of events will also charge a booth fee. You will probably have to supply your own tables or tent if it is outside. Do the same sort of calculations to see if a given fair is worth your time and expense. If it is, you can give away the same types of promotional materials.

Points to Remember

➤ There are book fairs of various sizes in every region of the country.

➤ Most book fairs charge a fee to be included. Calculate your expenses to determine if the fair is worth your time.

➤ Book fairs are excellent places to hand out promotional materials.

➤ Your publisher may have a booth at one of the larger fairs. Inquire if your book may be displayed.

➤ Make sure your book fits the fair's criteria.

➤ Local fairs and festivals may be a good choice to have a booth.

➤ You can find local fairs and festivals in your area by using the sites listed above.

Interviews

Strategy: Be in the public eye. Tell an audience about you and your book.

www.npr.org
www.ontheradio.net
www.tunein.com
www.radioguestlist.com
www.soulasylumpoetry.com

There are hundreds, if not thousands, of online podcasts and radio shows. Just search for "online radio" or "online talk show" to find a long list.

Hosts of talk shows are always looking for someone interesting to interview. You're a writer. You've written or done something interesting. You should be interviewed. The interview does not necessarily have to be about your book. Anything about you to get you on a show is worth talking about. These shows have international appeal.

Evaluate the sites one by one. You're looking for programs that interview people or review books. Some programs are only about books and writing. Find the contact information for the site. It's usually at the bottom of the home page. Send a message telling them who you are and why it would be interesting to their listeners to interview you. Use the same information you used when sending press releases.

National Public Radio, **NPR**, has a huge following across the country. They have shows specifically about books, most often the current best sellers. It's still worth a shot to write to them if you can give them a reason why interviewing you would be unique or interesting or thought provoking or engaging.

On The Radio gives a listing of radio stations and how to advertise on them. You don't necessarily want to advertise here, you want to get information about the listening audience of a particular station. This is useful if you're going to convince a talk show host to interview you.

Tune In is another place to find radio stations. They have a section for talk radio. Check it out to see if there is a station appropriate to your book.

Radio Guest List is similar to Help a Reporter except it is only for radio. Sign up to receive emails about topics the hosts are going to be using. Look at the menu on the left side of the page, and there is a "Sign up for Free Guest Available emails here" button. It will take you to the appropriate form.

If you are a poet, the **Soul Asylum** may be the place for you. It is poetry only and features books by poets. Although it is not a live broadcast, if you join the group you can find out how to become a featured author. Sort of an interview in print.

Points to Remember

➢ Talk radio hosts are always looking for interesting people to interview.

➢ Evaluate any radio station to make sure it is a fit for you and your book.

➢ Don't be shy about sending a message to be on a show.

➢ Use the same information and the approach you would for sending a press release.

Action Items
Miscellaneous

Date Completed   Item

_____   Check out TheNextBigWriter.com, Writ-ersCafe.com, CritiqueCircle.com.

_____   Check out Autocrit.com

_____   Check out Writer's Digest website list.

_____   Conduct a search to find magazines with your reader's demographics.

_____   Write and submit article to five print magazines.

_____   Write and submit article to five online magazines.

_____   Join ETSY and set up a shop.

_____   List book for sale in ETSY.

_____   Join eBay.

_____   List book for sale on eBay.

_____   Open a PayPal account.

_____   Research book reviewers and evaluate any possibilities.

_____   Research contact information for a celebrity endorsement.

_____   Write a letter to a celebrity and send it.

_____   Research contests and evaluate possible submission.

_____ Join Help a Reporter and sign up for emails.

_____ Research book fairs and evaluate any nearby.

_____ Research events and festivals. Evaluate the possibility of participating in one.

_____ Research online radio shows and pod-casts.

_____ Contact five shows or podcasts about being interviewed.

Putting It All Together

The methods presented here are not difficult to do. But they are time consuming. Schedule a little time each day to devote to something in this book. Amazon is the first thing you should tackle. Then you can select other items in order of their possible effectiveness.

Use this book as a log of what you do. The Action Items are ideal places to keep track of what you have tried and how effective it is. When you start a new strategy, review your current sales. Track sales daily and note any trend differences.

Many of the strategies are long term and are counter-intuitive to the traditional publishing industry methods. Traditional publishing puts all their effort in a book launch and if the book doesn't immediately take off they drop it and go on to another book.

Using the strategies in this book will allow you to continuously reach out to new groups of readers and generate interest months and even years after your published date.

Once you have the appropriate accounts set up, it is much easier to use your previous work to enhance a new strategy. Where you are in the publication process will dictate what actions you take first. Here are some suggested approaches.

Pre-publication

- ✓ Buy domain name for web site. Activate email account using your domain name. The web site does not have to be completely built in order to access associated email.

- ✓ Set up regular Amazon account for buying products using domain email.

- ✓ Create regular Goodreads, Shelfari, Library Thing and BookBub accounts using domain email. You're not ready to set up your author pages yet. Just get your accounts established.

- ✓ Join several writing web sites and vet your book with the experts at the site. Correct any problems.

- ✓ Either contract with someone to create your web site or set aside time to do it yourself.

- ✓ Send finished manuscript to any reviewers for any pre-publication reviews.

- ✓ Contact any potential celebrities or influential people for endorsement.

- ✓ Create ETSY and eBay accounts.

- ✓ Create Facebook, Linkedin, You Tube, Pinterest, and any other social media account you plan to use. Join appropriate groups.

- ✓ Create a Google account. Set up Google Alerts.

Book Launch/Publication

- ✓ Complete web site.

- ✓ Complete Author Central page. Assuming your book is activated, enter all author information. Put details of launch under "events."

- ✓ Announce date of the launch in all social media accounts.

- ✓ Write press release and send to local publications and any non-local publications that would be interested.

Post publication book signing

- ✓ Put details in your Author Central page on Amazon.
- ✓ Put details on your web site.
- ✓ Write a press release announcing the event.
- ✓ Announce event on your social media sites.
- ✓ Send press release to local publications.
- ✓ Send press release to appropriate press release distributors.
- ✓ Create fliers. Use QR code and give URL to your web site. Distribute in coffee shops, local bookstores, anywhere your readers might be.
- ✓ Create promotional handouts: bookmarkers with QR code, copies of first chapter, business cards, any signage to attract attention to yourself.

After the event, tally up your sales and the costs you incurred. Subtract costs from sales. Did you make a profit? If you did, consider duplicating the event in another place. If you didn't, consider concentrating your efforts on reaching readers on the internet.

Ongoing efforts

Spend an hour a day or more doing one of the activities listed. Do one strategy one day then another the next day to keep yourself interested.

- ✓ Give book away on Goodreads.
- ✓ Consider a BookBub giveaway.

- ✓ Research contests and enter an appropriate one. This should be done within the first year of publication.

- ✓ Create boards in Pinterest linked to your web page.

- ✓ Sell book on ETSY and eBay.

- ✓ Use search engine to find websites with similar interest and reach out to each one individually.

- ✓ Use search engine to find demographic groups and reach out to them individually.

- ✓ Sign up for publicity emails and evaluate them daily.

- ✓ Research book fairs, local fairs and any events where you might set up a table and sell your book.

- ✓ Create a Google Adwords campaign.

If you start a Google Adwords campaign, take note of sales before it starts and check them again about a month later. Can you see a difference? If the difference is not a positive one, with more royalty money in your pocket, shut down the campaign.

Many times it will be difficult to attribute sales to a specific effort. Marketing, by definition, is a collection of persuasive actions. Any resulting sale could be attributable to several things you have done.

Be patient and be dedicated. It may take some time for your efforts to be felt in the right places. It will pay off with more royalties and greater confidence as a writer.

Points to Remember

➢ This book can be used as a log to keep track of what you have tried and when.

➢ Customize the strategies in this book to your situation.

➢ Most of the strategies are long-term.

➢ These strategies will take time, but they are effective.

➢ Special events are opportunities for marketing your book. Use them to your advantage.

Final Thoughts

I know these strategies work because I have done them and have sold my book to a world-wide audience. They will work for you too. It may seem like a daunting task. The secret is to do a little at a time and not get overwhelmed.

Take a deep breath. You can do it.

Points to Remember

➢ YOU CAN DO IT!

R. C. Linnell Publishing

Consider using the publishing services of R. C. Linnell Publishing. We offer a unique business model that puts more royalties in your pocket.

We will format and publish your book, then turn everything over to you.

The process is quick and easy. A book ready for publication can be for sale on Amazon within a month.

Royalties go directly into your bank account, on a monthly basis.

www.LinnellPublishing.com

Other Books by Cheri Powell

Seven Tips to Make the Most of the Camino de Santiago

A book to help prospective pilgrims walk the 500 miles of the Camino de Santiago in northern Spain. Physical, mental, emotional, spiritual and logistical preparations are discussed.

The spiritual journey starts with you. This book will help you get there.

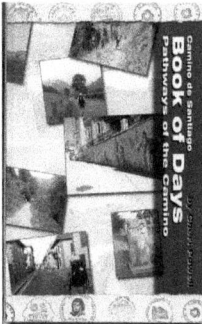

Camino de Santiago Book of Days Flowers of the Camino

A journal or date book with inspirational quotes and pictures of beautiful wildflowers along the Camino de Santiago.

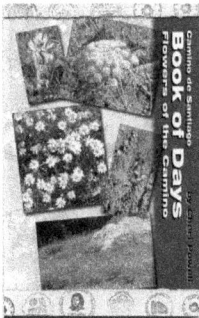

Camino de Santiago Book of Days Pathways of the Camino

A journal or date book with inspirational quotes and pictures of the path along the 500 mile trail of the Camino de Santiago.

Cheri Powell is available to speak to your group.

Marketing and Self-publishing

Talks or workshops can be customized to your group's needs. Cheri will lead you though the steps to market or self-publish your book.

Camino de Santiago

Cheri has walked the 500 miles of the Camino de Santiago twice. She gives inspirational talks and practical advice to prospective pilgrims and anyone interested in a spiritual journey.

Email for more information: Info@LinnellPublishing.com